# A Tribute to Mothers

EDITED BY Pat Mora

ILLUSTRATED BY Paula S. Barragán M.

LEE & LOW BOOKS Inc. • New York

*For my mother, Estela Delgado Mora,*
*in memory of my grandmother, Amelia Landavazo Delgado,*
*and my aunt, Ignacia Delgado; and for all who mother us*—P.M.

*For Matías and Bruno*—P.S.B.M.

Book Design by Christy Hale
Book Production by The Kids at Our House

The text is set in Latin 725
The illustrations are rendered in pencil, cut paper, and gouache
and then scanned into a computer and further designed with Adobe Illustrator.

Printed in Hong Kong by South China Printing Co. (1988) Ltd.
10  9  8  7  6  5  4  3  2  1
First Edition

Library of Congress Cataloging-in-Publication Data
Love to mamá : a tribute to mothers / edited by Pat Mora ;
illustrated by Paula S. Barragán M.— 1st ed.
p.   cm.     ISBN 1-58430-019-1
1. Mothers—Juvenile poetry. 2. Grandmothers—Juvenile poetry.
3. Children's poetry, American—Hispanic American authors. [1. Mothers—Poetry.
2. Grandmothers—Poetry. 3. Hispanic Americans—Poetry.
4. American poetry—Collections.] I. Mora, Pat. II. Barragán M., Paula S., ill.
PS595.M64 L68 2001
811'.60803520431—dc21     00-047787

# Introduction

When I was a little girl in El Paso, Texas, Mom cooked our meals, was president of the PTA, and helped Dad at his optical company. She was busy, but she loved to read and taught us to love books, too. Mom always helped my sisters, my brother, and me with homework. In English or Spanish, Mom could make words flow or fly and not go *clunk, clunk, clunk*. Mom also had a great sense of humor. Even when we worked hard together, we laughed and joked and had a good time.

My aunt, Ignacia Delgado, and my grandmother, Mamande, mothered us too. My tía read us books and told us stories in English and Spanish when we were in bed at night. I feel lucky that I grew up in a bilingual home. Mamande spoke only Spanish, so I learned the sweetness of the language from her. She brought us bowls of warm tomato soup to enjoy in bed when we were sick. Her soft hands always made us feel safe. Mothers, grandmothers, and special people do that, don't they?

Poems, like music, carry us to the deep feelings we hide inside. All the talented Latino poets in this book wrote to share their love for their mothers and grandmothers. The poets live in cities all over the country. Some have published many books before and others are new voices. All are proud to be Latino writers.

We hope you'll enjoy the beautiful illustrations by Paula Barragán and that you'll read and share these poems with people you love. Float on the music.

—PAT MORA

# Palomita

Wearing a sky-blue skirt
embroidered by an old woman
named Consuelo from a story
she told Mami a long time ago
on her island, a cuento
in gold, brown, and silver threads,
a shower of sunlight
falling like drops of gold on
a little golden girl
who turns into a silver dove
and flies around and around a blue sky,
my mami is walking with me in the park.
Palomita, palomita, is the name
she calls me, her little dove
happy to be going anywhere with her,
flying like a bird around and around
my mami in her sky-blue skirt
made from an island story.

JUDITH ORTIZ COFER

# The Race

She rode a horse named Fina
when women didn't ride.
They galloped around the mountain,
her legs on Fina's side.

She let her hair down from its bun
and felt it whip and fly.
She laughed and sang and whooped out loud.
Up there she wasn't shy!

One day great-grandma found her out
and planned to stop it all.
But down in town they'd heard some news . . .
they told her of a call.

A call for the caballeros
from all the highs and lows
to race their fancy caballos
to try and win the rose.

Abuela looked at Fina,
a twinkle in her eye.
Abuela said, "Let's enter!
This race deserves a try."

At dawn she was the only girl,
but didn't even care.
She came to meet the challenge, and
her horse was waiting there.

They swept across the finish line
much faster than the rest.
She flung her hat without surprise;
she'd always done her best.

Fina shook her mane and stomped.
Abuela flashed a smile.
She sniffed the rose and trotted off
in caballera style!

JENNIFER TRUJILLO

# Las abuelitas

When our grandmothers
come to visit, they bring us
gifts, regalitos, as they say

in Spanish, like sweet
caramelo. They bring us
stories from their childhoods

in Cuba when they too
were little girls, abuelita Nana,
abuelita Maña, cuentos

like the ones about giant gourd
trees and their smooth branches
curved low with moon-round gourds

they hit like piñatas, and the gourds
fell and cracked open, inside
a treasure of seeds

to make maracas rattle,
shake them to the beat of salsa music.
Las abuelitas cup their hands

to our ears like those dark gourds,
inside each, a little whisper
of our abuelitas' lives in Cuba.

VIRGIL SUÁREZ

# Growing Up

When I grow up,
I want to be a doctor.

*M'ija, you will patch scraped knees
and wipe away children's tears.*

But what if I become an architect?

*M'ija, you will build beautiful houses
where children will sing and play.*

And what if I become a teacher?

*M'ija, you will teach
your students to read every day.*

But what if I become a famous chef?

*M'ija, your arroz con pollo
will be eaten with gozo.*

And Mami, what if I want to be like you someday?

*M'ija, why do you want to be like me?*

Oh Mami, because you care for people, our house is built on love,
you are wise, and your spicy stew tastes delicious.


LIZ ANN BÁEZ AGUILAR

# Mi abuela

Most grandmothers wear aprons,
mi abuela likes to wear her leather skirt.
Many grandmothers like to bake cookies and cakes,
mi abuela likes to make tortillas y empanadas.
Some grandmothers enjoy reading and sewing,
mi abuela enjoys softball and my swings.
There are those grandmothers who make you chicken soup
when you are sick,
mi abuela makes me té de canela.
Other grandmothers like bingo,
mi abuela likes la lotería.
As you can see,
a mi abuelita le gusta la pura vida.

CRISTINA MUÑIZ MUTCHLER

# My Tongue Is Like a Map

Mami said yes, Abuelita sang sí.
They said, Two languages make you a rich man,
But words never paid for my penny candy.

Agua, water. Arroz, rice. Niño, me!
Arroz con leche, sang Abuelita
As my mami said, A is for Apple.

My ears were like a radio, so many stations.
Sometimes I would dream in English and Spanish.
I was a millionaire each time I said yes and sí.


RANE ARROYO

# I Helped My Mom
# Not to Be Late for Work

She was going to be late
for her first day of work,
and I was late for school.

But Mom couldn't say goodbye
to me and held me tightly in her arms,
kissing me in front of everyone.
I thought she was the only mother doing that.

She whispered in my ear that she was sad
to leave me and that she had to work.

I told her that I was in the first grade already,
strong like her and all grown up,
and then I dried the tears from her eyes,
opened my arms and let my mommy go.

CARMEN D. LUCCA

# Mi mamá cubana

When mi mamá cubana cooks arroz con pollo,
her smile is wider than a slice of watermelon.

Cutting green onions, the clucking tongue of mi mamá goes clicketty clack
Her silver bracelets slide up and down, jingling, jangling.

With a dash of saffron spice, mi mamá turns boiling rice bright yellow.
¡Ay! Sweet aroma of arroz con pollo carries me away.

Mi familia, we eat arroz con pollo, delicioso.
We sing "La cucaracha," con mucho gusto.
We dance mambo, tango, cha cha cha.

Closing my eyes I see palm trees swaying.
Seagulls circling. Haciendas, pink and green.

Still, sí sí, with eyes open I taste salty, saffron Cuba.
Muchas gracias, mamá cubana, for cooking up an island
in your tiny New York kitchen.

MIMI CHAPRA

# Mi abuelita es como
un nopal en flor

cada otoño
los nopales
de mi casa
y del barrio
se llenan
de tunas

mi abuelita
canta alegre
cuando pizca
las tunas que
ella sabe están
maduras y dulces

con tenazas
y cuchillo
mi abuelita
pela tunas
—las delicias
del desierto

como sabe que
estas suculencias
también son de veras
mi fruta favorita
mi abuelita me guiña
el ojo sin parar

# My Grandma Is Like
# a Flowering Cactus

every fall
the nopales
around my house
and neighborhood
are laden with
prickly pears

my grandma
sings with joy
when she picks
the prickly pears
she knows are
ripe and sweet

tongs and
knife in hand
my grandma
peels prickly pears
—the delicacies
of the desert

since she knows
these succulents
are also my favorite
fruits by far
my grandma can't
stop winking at me

FRANCISCO X. ALARCÓN

# Hidden in Abuelita's Soft Arms

Wrinkled and brown like an old paper bag,
Abuelita smiles with her too-perfect white teeth,
And she calls out as I run from Papa's old, gray station wagon,
"Mi cielo, come here! I need a big abrazo from you!"

And I bury myself deep, hidden in Abuelita's soft arms,
Smelling like perfume and frijoles and coffee and candy.

A whole weekend with Abuelita!
I shout, "Bye, Papa!"

Papa smiles and drives off in a puff of white smoke.
I bury my face deeper into her,
Just me and Abuelita,
For the whole weekend.

We march happily into her house
Painted yellow-white like a forgotten Easter egg,
And cracked here and there like that same egg.
But it is her home,
Near the freeway and St. Agnes Church.

On the wall there are pictures of Mama and my two aunts.
And there's one of Abuelita, so young and beautiful,
Standing close to Abuelito on their wedding day.

"Mi cielo," Abuelita says holding my sweaty cheeks in her
Cool, smooth hands.
"You are so big! My big boy!"
And I laugh and stand on my toes to be even bigger.

And I bury myself deep, hidden in Abuelita's soft arms,
Smelling like perfume and frijoles and coffee and candy.

DANIEL A. OLIVAS

# Abuelita Wears a Dress

Our jaws drop to our chests the evening
Abuelita steps out in a dress. Even the orange cat
glows its yellow eyes in surprise. Imagine that!
Abuelita waltzing out of the house in a shimmering

gray gown. Abuelita only wears pants and jeans.
Because she works all day in the grape
fields we think she has no shape
outside of a pair of old boots and green

flannel shirts. But there she stands, a silver-
colored moon of a woman ready to radiate
at my cousin's quinceañera. No pink cake
is as dazzling as Abuelita in heels.

And when la cumbia sways our hips across the floor,
Abuelita's bright red lipstick smile dances even more.


RIGOBERTO GONZÁLEZ

# My Grandmother Had One Good Coat

a black wool one with black buttons
shiny as patent leather shoes
and a smooth furry collar
just as black

she wore this only
to the doctor or to church

one late afternoon
I came home from school feeling sorry
for an old woman living beneath the
elevated train below the station
who sat taunting passersby
on their way to work and to school

she sat coatless on a cardboard box
hiding her pain behind
curses and scowls

she could have been
my own grandmother

and the thought of my own
grandmother homeless
in the cold with no place
to pray and be warm
made me sad and depressed

when she asked me what was wrong
and I told her without hesitation
she went into her closet
and handed me her black dress coat
and said here put it in a shopping
bag you'll find one in the broom closet
I don't use it that much anyway

TONY MEDINA

# Song to Mothers

Your laugh is a green song,
canción verde,
that branches
through our house,
its yellow blooms smelling
like warm honey.
Your laugh peels apples
and stirs their cinnamon bubblings,
then opens a book and pulls me
onto your lap.
At night, your laugh kisses
us soft as a petal, smooths my pillow
and covers me, a soft leafy blanket,
green and yellow.
I snuggle into your laugh,
your canción verde
and dream of growing
into my own green song.

PAT MORA

# About the Poets

**Liz Ann Báez Aguilar,** of Mexican descent, is an instructor of English at San Antonio College in New Mexico. Her short stories have appeared in *Kaleidoscope* and other journals. She is a native of San Antonio, New Mexico, where she currently lives.

**Francisco X. Alarcón,** a Chicano born in Wilmington, California, has written many award-winning children's books, including *Laughing Tomatoes and Other Spring Poems/Jitomates risueños y otros poemas de primavera,* and *From the Bellybutton of the Moon and Other Summer Poems/Del ombligo de la luna y otros poemas de verano,* both winners of the Pura Belpré Author Honor Award. A Danforth and Fulbright fellow, Alarcón currently teaches at and directs the Spanish for Native Speakers Program at the University of California, Davis. He lives in Davis.

**Rane Arroyo,** born in Chicago, Illinois, is an award-winning Puerto Rican poet. He won the Carl Sandburg Poetry Prize for his book of poems, *The Singing Shark,* and the Pushcart Prize for his poem, *Breathing Lessons.* Arroyo is Associate Chair at the University of Toledo's Department of English where he teaches Creative Writing. He lives in Toledo, Ohio.

**Mimi Chapra,** a native of Havana, Cuba, is a writer, painter, and sculptor with degrees in Fine Arts and English Literature. She has written for children's magazines and her book for beginning readers has been published by Bebop Books, an imprint of Lee & Low. She currently lives in Philadelphia, Pennsylvania.

**Judith Ortiz Cofer,** a native of Hormigueros, Puerto Rico, is a widely published poet, novelist, essayist, and short story writer for children and adults. Her collection of short stories, *An Island Like You: Stories of the Barrio,* was an American Library Association Best Book of the Year and the winner of the first Pura Belpré Author Award. Cofer is also a professor of English and Creative Writing at the University of Georgia in Athens. She lives in Athens.

**Rigoberto González,** born in Bakersfield, California, is a Chicano poet and writer whose first book of poetry, *So Often the Pitcher Goes to Water Until It Breaks,* was published as part of the National Poetry Series. A Guggenheim fellow, he is also a winner of the John Guyon Prize for literary nonfiction. He currently lives in New York City, where he is a bilingual literacy teacher in Brooklyn.

**Carmen D. Lucca,** a native of Ponce, Puerto Rico, is a poet whose work has appeared in *Brushstrokes and Landscapes* and other anthologies. In addition to being a writer, she has been a bilingual teacher in New York City for over 20 years. She lives in the Bronx.

**Tony Medina,** of Black Puerto Rican descent, is a native of the South Bronx. He is a poet whose first book of poetry for children, *DeShawn Days,* was published by Lee & Low. He was selected as one of 10 poets to watch in the new millennium by *Writer's Digest.* Medina is also a professor of English at Long Island University and lives in New York City.

**Pat Mora,** a Mexican American born in El Paso, Texas, is the author of numerous award-winning books for adults and children, including *Tomás and the Library Lady, This Big Sky,* and Lee & Low's *Confetti: Poems for Children.* Her memoir, *House of Houses,* reveals her interest in family and her Chicano heritage. She is also a university professor, popular speaker, and children's advocate who helped establish April 30th as Día de los niños/Día de los libros, a yearly celebration of childhood, books, languages, and cultures. Mora lives in Edgewood, Kentucky, and Santa Fe, New Mexico.

**Cristina Muñiz Mutchler,** of Mexican and German descent, is 15 years old and the anthology's youngest poet. In addition to keeping up with her schoolwork, Mutchler co-hosts a local Emmy award-winning children's television program, *Zoo Today.* She lives in Toledo, Ohio.

**Daniel A. Olivas** is a Chicano writer from Los Angeles, California, whose fiction has appeared in numerous literary journals and an anthology. In addition to being a writer, he is the Deputy Attorney General at the California Department of Justice. He lives in Los Angeles.

**Virgil Suárez,** born in Havana, Cuba, has published numerous novels, short stories, essays, and poetry for adults, including *Spared Angola: Memories from a Cuban-American Childhood, The Cutter,* and *In the Republic of Longing.* A part-time professor at Florida State University, he lives in Tallahassee and Key Biscayne, Florida.

**Jennifer L. Trujillo,** a writer of Venezuelan descent, was raised in her birth place, Denver, Colorado, and in Caracas, Venezuela. A winner of the *Latina* magazine essay contest, Trujillo currently teaches at Fort Lewis College in Durango, and at the Navajo Indian Reservation in Cortez. She lives in Durango, Colorado.

## About the Illustrator

**Paula S. Barragán M.** is a native of Quito, Ecuador. She received her degree in graphic design and illustration from Pratt Institute in Brooklyn, New York. In addition to being a painter, Barragán is a printmaker and carpet designer. Her fine art pieces are shown at galleries in the United States and South America. Barragán currently lives in Quito. This is her first picture book.

# Glossary

A mi abuelita le gusta la pura vida (**AH MEE ah-bweh-LEE-tah LEH GOOS-tah LAH POO-rah BEE-dah**): My grandma enjoys the good life

Abuela (**ah-BWEH-lah**): Grandmother

Abuelita (**ah-bweh-LEE-tah**): Grandma

Abuelito (**ah-bweh-LEE-toh**): Grandpa

Abrazo (**ah-BRAH-soh**): Hug

Agua (**AH-gwah**): Water

Arroz (**ah-RROHS**): Rice

Arroz con leche (**ah-RROHS KOHN LEH-cheh**): Rice pudding

Arroz con pollo (**ah-RROHS KOHN POH-yoh**): Rice with chicken

Caballeros (**kah-bah-YEH-rohs**): Men who ride horses, also means "gentlemen"

Caballera style (**kah-bah-YEH-rah**): In the style of a female rider

Caballos (**kah-BAH-yohs**): Horses

Canción verde (**kahn-SYOHN BEHR-deh**): Green song

Caramelo (**kah-rah-MEH-loh**): Caramel or hard candy

Cha cha cha (**chah chah CHAH**): Cuban dance rhythm

Con mucho gusto (**KOHN MOO-choh GOOS-toh**): With great pleasure

Cuento/s (**KWEN-toh/tohs**): Story/ies

Cumbia (**KOOM-byah**): A dance rhythm popular in Mexico and throughout Latin America

Delicioso (**deh-lee-SYOH-soh**): Delicious

Frijoles (**free-HOH-lehs**): Beans

Gozo (**GOH-soh**): Pleasure

Haciendas (**ah-SYEHN-dahs**): Large ranches

La cucaracha (**LAH koo-kah-RAH-chah**): A popular children's song, also a traditional Mexican revolutionary song; literally means "the cockroach"

Lotería (**loh-teh-REE-ah**): Board game similar to bingo

Mamá (**mah-MAH**): Mother

Mambo (**MAHM-boh**): Afro-Cuban musical form

Mami (**MAH-mee**): Mom

Maracas (**mah-RAH-kahs**): Hand-held rattles or shakers

Mi cielo (**MEE SYEH-loh**): Term of endearment, "my dear;" literally means "my sky"

Mi familia (**MEE fah-MEE-lyah**): My family

M'ija (**MEE-hah**): Affectionate form of "mi hija" which means "my daughter"

Muchas gracias (**MOO-chahs GRAH-syahs**): Thank you very much

Nopales (**noh-PAHL-ehs**): Prickly pears

Niño (**NEE-nyoh**): Boy

Palomita (**pah-loh-MEE-tah**): Term of endearment, "little dove"

Papá (**pah-PAH**): Dad

Piñatas (**pee-NYAH-tahs**): Colored paper figures that usually hold candy inside

Quinceañera (**keen-seh-ah-NYEH-rah**): A party given when a girl turns 15 years old

Regalitos (**reh-gah-LEE-tohs**): Small gifts

Salsa (**SAHL-sah**): Popular Latin music with roots in Afro-Cuban music

Sí (**SEE**): Yes

Té de canela (**TEH DEH kah-NEH-lah**): Cinnamon tea

Tía (**TEE-ah**): Aunt

Tortillas y empanadas (**tohr-TEE-yahs EE ehm-pah-NAH-dahs**): "Tortillas" are rounded and flattened pieces of dough made of flour or corn; "empanadas" are turnovers with a flaky crust and a savory filling

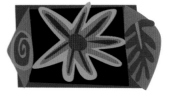